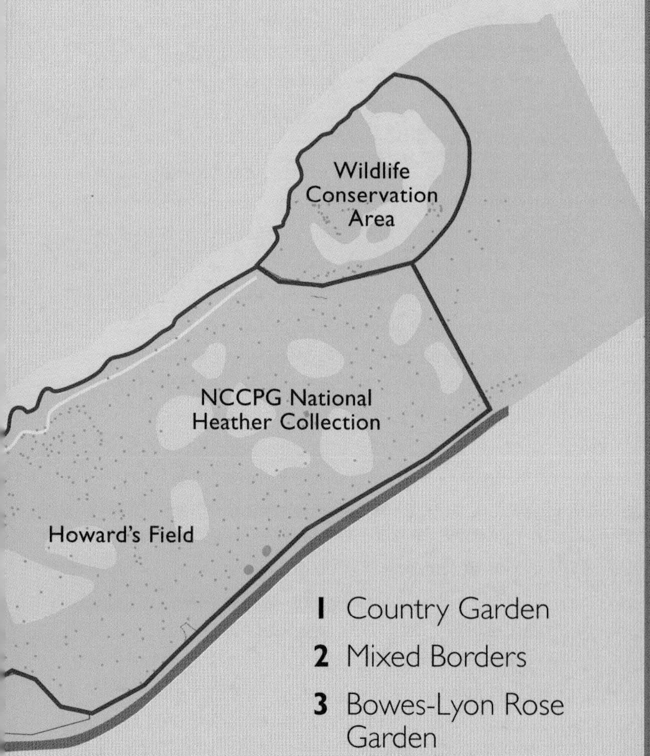

Wildlife Conservation Area

NCCPG National Heather Collection

Howard's Field

1 Country Garden

2 Mixed Borders

3 Bowes-Lyon Rose Garden

4 Model Gardens

5 Herb Garden

6 Fruit Demonstration Garden

7 Alpine Display Houses

8 Model Vegetable Garden

9 Rock Garden

10 Alpine Meadow

11 Walled Gardens

12 Canal & Loggia

13 Members' Advisory Service

14 Garden Library

15 Laboratory

16 Glasshouse

Contents

Welcome

Seven Acres Daffodils (*Narcissus* 'Toto') and grape hyacinths (*Muscari armeniacum*) beneath spring-flowering shrubs *Exochorda racemosa* (*foreground*) and *E. giraldii* (*above centre right*)

RHS Garden Wisley is undoubtedly one of the great gardens of the world. It is said 'if it can grow at Wisley, then it can grow anywhere'. Our plant collections here, approaching 30,000 taxa, are some of the largest in the world. What makes the collections unique is their diversity. Nowhere else can you find one of the most comprehensive collections of fruit growing beside glasshouse plants, alpines and vegetables, as well as conventional collections of bulbs, herbaceous and woody plants.

Yet Wisley is far more than just a collection of plants: it is a source of inspiration and education. The Broadwalk is an example of gardening on the grand scale: it lies between two 128m-long mixed borders that display a wealth of ideas for intriguing plant associations. Why not compare the traditional use of herbaceous plants in the Mixed Borders with the lower-maintenance, prairie-style planting in the Glasshouse Borders? You can inspect alpine plants in flower at close quarters on every day of the year in the Alpine Display Houses or find design, planting and cultivation ideas for smaller-scale gardens in the demonstration and model gardens, such as Witan Street. In our magnificent new Glasshouse, you can immerse yourself in the wonders of desert, rainforest or tropical plants, marvel at the intricate blooms of the many orchids on display, find out the secrets of plant roots or learn about the skills needed to cultivate the Teaching Garden.

Wisley is also a centre of education where gardeners of all ages can acquire horticultural skills. Each year, students from around the world join our Horticultural Training Programme and study for the Diploma in Practical Horticulture or one of six one-year Specialist Certificates. Working with trained staff provides the students with the practical skills that they will need. The skills of the professional gardeners are also passed on to RHS members, who benefit from attending demonstrations and garden walks that cover a diversity of topics. Wisley is also a garden where children and their teachers can learn about plants and get hands-on practical experience, linking many aspects of their garden visits directly to the National Curriculum.

CULTIVATING THE GARDEN

There are over 90 staff looking after the garden itself; they include support staff who deal with mapping, plant records and labelling, information services, collecting and distributing seed, machinery, tree management, irrigation and turf care. As well as being a great unifying element, the grass in the garden varies tremendously,

Glasshouse Borders The frosted perennial seedheads and grasses in this prairie-style planting provide a fine approach to the Glasshouse in winter

from the beautifully manicured lawns by the Canal and Laboratory to the long grass of the Alpine Meadow, which is a wildlife habitat as well as home to thousands of spring-flowering, hoop-petticoat daffodils.

SOIL AND CLIMATE

We have kept meteorological records since 1904; they show that the garden temperatures vary between 30°C and −10°C, with extremes of 37.8°C in August 2003 and −15°C in January 1982. June and July are our sunniest months, with an all-time high of 294 sunshine hours in June 1975. The long-term average rainfall is 646.7mm per year although in 2000, one of our wettest years, it was 958.9mm. We experienced our driest April (1.8mm) and wettest July (174.4mm) ever recorded, in 2007.

The soil at Wisley is generally an acidic, free-draining, sandy loam, with a natural soil pH of 5.5. With frequent cultivation, the pH has risen above neutral and become slightly alkaline. To maintain plants in top condition on this free-draining soil, it is important to have an effective irrigation system. We ensure that water is used wisely with 20km of underground irrigation pipes, using rainwater harvested from roofs, a borehole and water from the River Wey. Data from 22 recently installed, soil-moisture measurement points also helps us to target irrigation efficiently and to plant appropriately in the garden.

Glasshouse The Queen opened the Glasshouse officially on 26 June 2007 and was escorted on a tour of the area by RHS President Peter Buckley

LOOKING TO THE FUTURE

Running the garden at Wisley demands both long-term vision and shorter-term development programmes, as we strive to demonstrate horticultural practice of the highest order that is both up-to-date and relevant to visitors. Maintaining such horticultural excellence depends on the many committed and well-trained professional gardeners and trainees who enjoy working in the garden; the input from our many volunteers is also highly valued.

The Society's aspirations for all its gardens are ambitious: accordingly, we have embarked on a long-term planning and development process that aims to build on Wisley's standing as a horticultural centre of international significance and major year-round recreational attraction. We need to accommodate rising numbers of visitors and make more provision for families and children, while preserving the garden's unique character and environmental credentials. This great garden has steadily evolved over the past 100 years and we hope that you will share our excitement as you see the changes undertaken to fulfil this next challenging phase in the garden's development. We want to ensure that each visit, whether during the depths of winter or on a bright summer's day, is a special day for you and that you will be inspired, informed and delighted.

Choice cultivar Wisley offers the opportunity to see and enjoy thousands of different plants, such as this *Dahlia* 'Nargold', and to pick up ideas for plant associations in a garden setting

Jim Gardiner
Curator, RHS Garden Wisley

Canal area

Framing the entrance to Wisley are ornate wrought-iron gates displaying the date of the Society's founding in 1804. They commemorate the Rev. William Wilks, who gave us the well-known Shirley poppies – also part of the gate design. Directly in front of the gates is a stone bird bath. Touch its base stone and you

Canal This view, from the Laboratory, looks towards the Loggia and the Conifer Lawn beyond it

are touching a part of the original Waterloo Bridge, which once spanned the River Thames in London; the bridge was replaced with a newer version. Turn right after the gates to go towards the Canal.

THE LABORATORY

The half-timbered, Surrey-style building known as the Laboratory is the focal point of the garden. The Laboratory was purpose built in 1914–16 to accommodate the Society's scientific staff and house a lecture theatre and classrooms for the School of Horticulture (*see p46*). Today it provides office accommodation for the administrative and scientific staff, as well as a small lecture theatre and classroom (surviving from the original 1903 building). These are primarily used for general horticultural lectures and demonstrations attended by RHS members and the public.

Weathervane This was designed specifically for the new Loggia in 1970; it incorporates a golden cloud with raindrop insets

CANAL & LOGGIA

In 1969–70, the Canal was redeveloped to formal designs by the distinguished landscape architects Sir Geoffrey Jellicoe and Lanning Roper. The formal water feature is bordered by immaculate lawns; a simple cascade and an elegant fountain soothe the air and aerate the water. The open-sided Loggia at the end of the canal – formerly the potting shed – supports a magnificent *Wisteria floribunda*. It also offers an excellent point to view one of the largest collections of waterlilies (*Nymphaea*) on one stretch of water in the UK. Throughout summer, the south-facing border on one side of the Canal is filled with perennials and half-hardy plants, which thrive in this open, sunny site. On the other side, shrubby plantings in raised beds frame the edge of the Conifer Lawn.

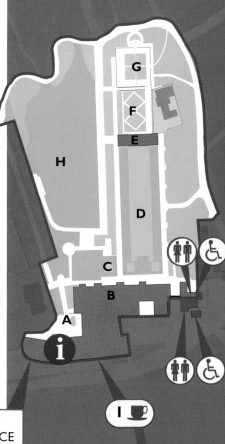

GARDEN ENTRANCE

Carpet bedding Displays of bedding plants, such as *Alternanthera*, at the foot of the Canal, carry on a tradition that was established in Victorian public parks

Laboratory Although it was built after the RHS acquired the garden, the building sits very comfortably in its garden setting

CANAL AREA

A	Wilks Gates
B	Laboratory
C	Carpet bedding
D	Canal
E	Loggia
F	Walled Garden East
G	Walled Garden West
H	Conifer Lawn
I	Coffee Shop

Highlights

» Summer: waterlilies in Canal

» Late spring–autumn: choice planting and formal parterre in Walled Gardens

» Summer–autumn: carpet bedding

» Year-round: Conifer Lawn

Canal area

Warm wall A fine example of the double-flowered *Wisteria floribunda* 'Yae-kokuryú' (often mistakenly labelled as 'Black Dragon') enjoys the heat from the wall facing the Conifer Lawn

Walled Garden West The informal planting in this garden creates a lush, tropical atmosphere – some of the plants are changed each year but usually combine bold foliage, such as that of *Phormium tenax*, with flowers of hot hues, as in *Pelargonium quercifolium*

WALLED GARDENS

The 3m-tall walls that enclose the two Walled Gardens provide shelter – much needed since Wisley can be prone to damaging frosts during winter and spring. In the rear Walled Garden West, these high walls create a microclimate that enables tender and subtropical plants to survive. Over 30 per cent of the permanent plants, such as palms and ferns, are tender. Redesigned and replanted in 2001 with the support of Witan Investment Trust plc, this informal garden illustrates how to mix hardy and tender plants from around the world in a modern setting, and it has become a plantsman's corner. Visit Wisley in winter to see how the more tender exotics, such as ornamental bananas (*Musa basjoo*), are carefully wrapped to shield them from the worst of the weather and winter wet.

In the Walled Garden East, nearest the canal, massed plantings are laid out as a formal parterre in a variety of spring and summer bedding schemes, creating a vibrant pattern of colour that is visible from inside the Laboratory building.

CONIFER LAWN

In the early days of the garden at Wisley, a small pinetum was planted directly opposite the Laboratory. Today only a few specimens remain: some have been lost to storms, some to old age or disease, but among those left are mature specimens of the yellow *Chamaecyparis lawsoniana* 'Lutea' and the stately cedar of Lebanon (*Cedrus libani*). Development plans for this area include new planting and an opening up of the vistas from the lawn.

Conifer Lawn Some of these majestic conifers are about 100 years old and are the last survivors of some of the earliest plantings at Wisley, although the cedar (*above left*) is only 30–40 years old

Walled Garden East (*Right*) Formal planting rings the changes, with massed bulbs in spring (*main image*) to summer annuals such as golden-yellow *Rudbeckia hirta* 'Indian Summer' (*inset*)

Central area

The central area of the garden contains some of the most intricate and ornamental floral displays to be seen outdoors at Wisley. Peak seasons for these mostly mixed and herbaceous plantings are spring, summer and autumn, so they are worth visiting at several times of the year to see what's new.

Seedheads *Allium cristophii* flowers in the Mixed Borders in late spring and then offers attractive seedheads, here with *Molinia caerulea* subsp. *caerulea*

Long-lasting colour (*Below*) The large daisies of *Echinacea purpurea* sing out from the Mixed Borders from midsummer through to early autumn

MIXED BORDERS

Chief among the glories of Wisley are the Mixed Borders, which run either side of the Broadwalk, on the slope leading up to Battleston Hill. The borders are 128m long and 6m wide and backed by hornbeam hedges. They are designed to be viewed along their entire lengths, when the full impact of the massed plantings may be best appreciated.

A rich diversity of plants in the borders offers plenty of interest and an impressive display that lasts from late spring to autumn, but the planting reaches its peak during July and August. Composition is paramount and is achieved through graded colour schemes and variations in textures and height. The Society's aim is to excite and inspire visitors to try similar plant associations in their own gardens.

Summer heat Hot colours combine in the Mixed Borders with *Helenium* 'Bruno' (*left in foreground*), bold-leaved *Canna* 'Phasion' and *Helenium* 'Sonnenwunder' (*centre*), and the tall grass *Miscanthus sinensis* 'Zebrinus'

Staking perennials Tall perennials provide much of the colour throughout summer and autumn in the Mixed Borders. In our gardens, such perennials can be badly affected by rain and wind and, to keep a border looking as glorious as those at Wisley, it is important to support the plants as unobtrusively as possible. Several techniques for staking, such as using peasticks (from birch stems), netting, wire cylinders and obelisks, are employed in the borders. The supports are put in place early in the season, as growth begins, so that all the staking is soon camouflaged by foliage. This technique is essential to the success of the borders.

LATE SUMMER BORDERS

Running at right angles to the Mixed Borders are two herbaceous borders, which have been designed to blaze with colour in late summer and autumn. Plants include asters, Japanese anemones, Korean chrysanthemums, penstemons and sedums.

Highlights

» Spring–autumn: Mixed Borders, Country Garden, bedding in Top Terrace

» Summer: roses

» Late summer–autumn: Late Summer Borders

Late Summer Borders Hardy 'Korean' chrysanthemums have masses of vividly coloured flowers to bring colour to the borders from late summer to autumn

Central area

COUNTRY GARDEN

Many gardeners have the problem of what to do with a sloping site. When faced with this challenge while designing the Country Garden, Penelope Hobhouse chose to create three horizontal areas on different levels, linking them with sloping paths to ensure wheelchair access.

Avenues of crab apple trees (*Malus* × *zumi* 'Professor Sprenger' and *M. hupehensis*) flank both sides of the garden, providing shade as well as creating height and alleviating the flatness of the terracing. Eight 3m-tall pergolas also draw the eye and support climbing plants. The surrounding plantings are largely herbaceous perennials and bulbs, with some shrubs. Through the growing season, the predominant colours change from misty blues, pinks and whites to glowing yellows, oranges and rusts in late summer.

The hard landscape layout is formal, but is softened by the informality of the planting. Plants derived from similar habitats and with the same cultural requirements grow close together in a cottage-garden style. Many of the plant associations used here could be adopted in smaller, domestic gardens.

Apple avenues Formally trained crab apples, *Malus* × *zumi* 'Professor Sprenger' and *M. hupehensis*, in the Country Garden are laden with spring blossom and later bright fruits

GOLDEN JUBILEE ROSE GARDEN

To celebrate the Golden Jubilee in 2002 of the Society's patron, HM Queen Elizabeth II, a new rose garden was designed to replace the old 'garden for new rose introductions' at Wisley. The central focus of the new scheme remains roses of mixed types that are new to cultivation; examples of all the main types of rose, from shrub and modern English to climbing and floribunda roses, can be studied here. Narrow beds set in turf also make it easy to get up close and smell the roses.

Choice blooms
In the borders of the Golden Jubilee Rose Garden, you can see cultivars such as Hyde Hall (*left*) and Elina (*far left*)

In the Rose Garden (*Above*)
Standard roses of White Diamond in midsummer flower above salmon-peach Razzle Dazzle and the unusual shades of Rhapsody in Blue

Country Garden (*Left*) In high summer, cool blues and purples predominate, in the flowers of herbaceous perennials such as delphiniums (*centre*) and *Linaria purpurea* (*foreground*)

Battleston Hill

The acid soil at Wisley is ideal for plants such as rhododendrons, camellias, magnolias and azaleas. The original plantings on Battleston Hill were made in 1937, but vast areas were replanted after the storms of 1987 and 1990 laid flat much of the tree canopy. Between April and June, the vibrant colours of the

azaleas and rhododendrons make Battleston Hill a magnet for all visitors. Particular collections of rhododendrons include: hardy hybrids; R. *yakushimanum* hybrids, which are low-growing, hardy, floriferous and ideal for a small garden; evergreen azaleas; Kurume azaleas, introduced in 1918 from Japan by the famous plant collector E H Wilson and considered by him to be 'the loveliest of all Azaleas'; and deciduous azaleas, many of them sweetly scented with lovely autumn foliage.

The hill has numerous, winding footpaths and woody planting to provide interest throughout the year, including camellias, hydrangeas, mahonias and pieris, with large groups of herbaceous plants such as agapanthus, day lilies (*Hemerocallis*), hostas, lilies and meconopsis. Numerous acers have been planted for autumn colour. Winter reveals the beauties of bark, on trees such as birch (*Betula*), chestnut (*Castanea*), oak (*Quercus*) and stewartias, as well as tantalising scents from winter-

Spring *Magnolia* x *soulangeana* 'Rustica Rubra' is one of many fine examples of this genus growing on Battleston Hill

Late summer View walking southeast towards the brow of the hill, past the blue blooms of agapanthus and white flower spikes of *Hydrangea paniculata*

Beautiful bark Many trees, like this eucalyptus in the Mediterranean Garden, have attractively coloured or textured bark

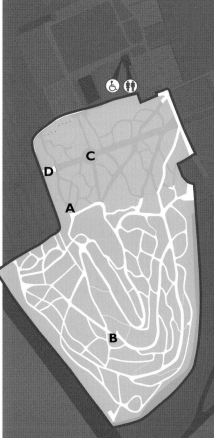

flowerers such as daphnes and witch hazels (*Hamamelis*). There are also some snowdrops from the NCCPG National *Galanthus* Collection (*see p39*) to be seen on the hill in late winter. At the top of the main hill, a large sculpture, changed every few years, acts as a dramatic focal point.

MEDITERRANEAN GARDEN
In the hottest part of the garden, on the south side of the hill, is a collection of sun-loving plants from the Mediterranean, Australasia, California and South Africa. These plants thrive in the sharply draining, sandy soil on this sloping bank. Collections of brooms (*Genista*), Californian lilac (*Ceanothus*), eucalyptus, gazanias, rock roses (*Cistus*), and sages (*Salvia*) all brighten this sunny corner of the garden.

BATTLESTON HILL

A	Mediterranean Garden
B	Battleston Hill East
C	Viewpoint
D	Steps to Trials Field

Highlights

» Spring–early summer: azaleas, hostas, magnolias and rhododendrons

» Summer: herbaceous and Mediterranean plants

» Autumn foliage

» Winter: bark and scent including witch hazels (*Hamamelis*), part of NCCPG National *Galanthus* Collection

Rhododendrons (*Left*) In spring, the hill is a mass of colour, some of it from slow-growing hybrid rhododendrons such as the red-flowered 'Hinode-no-taka' and cream-flowered 'Carita Inchmery' (*foreground*) and a white form of *R. campanulatum* (*background right*)

Trials Field

Since the installation of its first trial grounds at the Chiswick garden (see *p44*), plant trials have formed and continue to form an important element of the Society's work. In the Trials Field, plants are grown specifically in order to compare the different cultivars available and to assess their merits and worthiness for garden use.

Rosewarne Collection Groups of daffodils from the collection in the north-western corner of the Trials Field

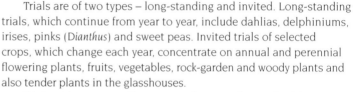

Trials are of two types – long-standing and invited. Long-standing trials, which continue from year to year, include dahlias, delphiniums, irises, pinks (*Dianthus*) and sweet peas. Invited trials of selected crops, which change each year, concentrate on annual and perennial flowering plants, fruits, vegetables, rock-garden and woody plants and also tender plants in the glasshouses.

Trial entries are usually grown under a number and cultivar name, and a detailed record of their performance is kept by the Trials Office. Information boards, listing names of the entries, cultivation processes and objectives of the trial, are displayed adjacent to each trial. All plants are assessed by the appropriate RHS committees, members of which may often be observed in the Trials Field while carrying out their duties. The prestigious Award of Garden Merit (*see opposite*) may be bestowed on a plant according to their recommendations.

THE NCCPG NATIONAL PLANT COLLECTION

Rhubarb The NCCPG National Plant Collection of rhubarb held at Wisley is one of the oldest National Plant Collections (*see p51*) in the

Summer colour The various trials, such as this one of busy Lizzies (*Impatiens walleriana*), form a bright patchwork of colour across the field

Vegetable bed
Some vegetables are trialled in the field, such as these cos and semi-cos lettuces

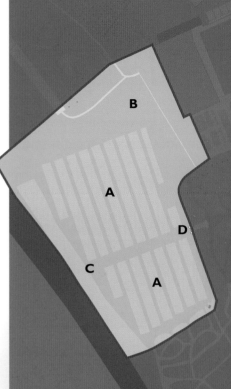

UK. It was begun at the Society's former garden at Chiswick and transferred to Wisley in 1904. Since then, new introductions have been added and the collection now numbers 151 cultivars, including 12 ornamental varieties. Another National Plant Collection of rhubarb is kept at the RHS Garden Harlow Carr, in Yorkshire.

The rhubarbs at Wisley are grown together in a single bed on the Trials Field, where their differences may be compared. Each year, detailed records are kept of growth habits from bud burst to maturity. All the cultivars have been photographed as cut stems; these images may be used to show the characteristics of individual cultivars and so help resolve any queries. Every three years, the collection is divided and surplus stocks distributed to collection holders and, through the Wisley Plant Centre, to the public.

Award of Garden Merit

Intended as a practical guide for the ordinary gardener, the Award of Garden Merit (AGM) is granted only to plants that are:

» excellent for ordinary garden use
» available
» of good constitution
» essentially stable in form and colour
» reasonably resistant to pests and diseases
» reasonably easy to grow.

There are currently over 7,000 AGM plants; new awards are made each year to keep the list as up-to-date as possible. The complete list may be found on the RHS website (www.rhs.org.uk/plants/award_plants.asp).

General enquiries about the AGM may be sent to:
AGM Lists, Botany Dept, RHS Garden Wisley, Woking, Surrey GU23 6QB or email: agmaward@rhs.org.uk

Aster × frikartii 'Wunder von Stäfa'

Iris ensata 'Barr Purple East'

TRIALS FIELD

A Trials beds
B Rosewarne Collection
C Pavilion
D Steps to Mediterranean garden on Battleston Hill

Highlights

» Spring: bulbs, early vegetables
» Summer: annuals, biennials & perennials, fruits & vegetables
» Autumn: chrysanthemums, dahlias

Rheum × hybridum 'Timperley Early'

Model Gardens

Created specifically with the needs of the average home gardener in mind, the model gardens present a catalogue of practical design ideas and show how you can have something of interest in the garden throughout four seasons. The displays in the 18 model gardens are all on the scale of a domestic plot

and have been designed by a variety of garden designers or by Wisley staff and students. Also in this area, you can see the Subtropical Borders, which are planted each year with a new display. Nearby is the site of the decommissioned glasshouses, which will be undergoing redevelopment over the next few years.

Daily Telegraph Reflective Garden Originally awarded Best Garden in Show at the 1999 Chelsea Flower Show, this garden was designed by Michael Balston. Modern tensile fabrics and gleaming steel masts contrast modern sculptural forms with traditional planting. A dry 'river bed' of pebbles runs through the richly textural foliage.

Town Garden This scheme was opened in 2001 and sponsored by A W Champion Ltd. It has been refreshed since and features a range of timber products including decking, seating, a garden house and modern fencing. The contemporary style of the garden is enhanced by a sculptural glass water feature and the choice of planting.

Garden of Rooms The Agriframes Garden of Rooms, designed by Ann Kennedy, contains supports, arches and pergolas clothed in a diverse collection of climbers and wall plants, to demonstrate how a garden can be divided into intimate areas.

Family Garden Designed by Fiona Lawrenson and funded by the National Garden Scheme, this garden was constructed in 2004. It integrates relaxed and formal areas with a number of functions, such as a patio and a play area, so that the garden can be enjoyed by all members of the family. Planting is also varied, with drought-tolerant plants in gravel, herbaceous borders, alpines and shade-lovers.

Subtropical Borders (*Right*) These borders are planted in spring with bulbs (*top*). Tender perennials and annuals, chosen for bold foliage and flamboyant flowers, pack the borders with a lush summer display (*centre*). In autumn, most of the plants are lifted, but larger plants, such as bananas, are packed with straw (*bottom*) to insulate them over winter

Container Garden (*Right*) Grasses in pots provide a long-lasting foil to plants grown as annuals for summer colour

Family Garden Year-round structure is provided in this garden by pleached hornbeams (*Carpinus betulus*), which contrast with the softer outlines of box, lavenders and grasses beneath

MODEL GARDENS

A	*Daily Telegraph* Reflective Garden
B	Town Garden
C	Garden of Rooms
D	Family Garden
E	Container Garden
F	Enthusiast's Garden
G	*Evening Standard* Eros Garden
H	Bonsai Garden
I	Subtropical Borders
J	Witan Street
K	Witan Investment Trust Model Herb Garden
L	Fruit Demonstration Gardens
M	Orchard Café (seasonal opening)
N	Hillside Events Centre

Highlights

» Spring: bulbs in Subtropical Borders

» Summer: Subtropical Borders

» Spring–autumn: all gardens

» Year-round: Reflective, Family, Container, Enthusiast's, Bonsai gardens

Container Garden Anyone with a patio or small paved garden will be inspired by this collection of containers filled with a range of annuals, perennials and bulbs. The display is changed regularly to demonstrate the versatility of container planting, as well as plant associations with different permutations of colour and texture. You can also see one of Wisley's bird stations in this garden.

Enthusiast's Garden Designed by Robin Williams, this well established garden focuses on design and planting associations, using a wide variety of interesting plants, and offers plenty of ideas for the keen and enthusiastic gardener. It is scheduled to be replaced in the near future.

Model Gardens

***Evening Standard* Eros Garden** After winning a silver medal at the 1995 Chelsea Flower Show, this garden was installed at Wisley in 1996. It illustrates timelessly just what can be achieved in a small courtyard garden. Look for the trained whitebeams (*Sorbus aria*) that form the gazebo and gate arch.

Bonsai Garden This garden has been sponsored by Dawn and Peter Chan of Herons Bonsai Nursery since 1998; it was completely remade in March 2007 and opened by the Japanese Ambassador and Peter Buckley, President of the RHS, in July 2007. The Japanese garden and collection of bonsai illustrate the ancient art with bonsai trees of the highest quality. They include rare Japanese maples, junipers and pines, some of which are over a hundred years old. It is very colourful when the maples (*Acer*) burst into leaf, but the Zen style of the garden makes it a particularly serene space, even in winter.

Bonsai Garden The container-grown bonsai trees are raised on plinths so that their miniature forms may be more easily appreciated; larger bonsai trees are planted in the garden

WITAN STREET

The RHS, in collaboration with the Society of Garden Designers, installed this 'street' of eight gardens between 2004 and 2008. The plots are all the same small size (9 x 6m) and are designed to reflect

No.4 Witan Street 'Intersection' by Catherine Heatherington inspired by the backdrop of pine trees and has blocks of evergreen box and yew

No.5 Witan Street 'Development' by Paul Dracott is a drought-tolerant garden planted with grasses and foliage plants such as *Festuca glauca*

Herb Garden The design is based on threes: there are three entrances, outer areas and central circles around the sundial, which is shaped like an astrolabe

modern lifestyles and attitudes to gardening. Whether contemporary or traditional in approach, they all provide exciting and instructive examples of low-maintenance gardens. Each model garden will be exhibited for at least four years before being replaced, so that the street will continue to showcase new ideas and planting styles.

WITAN INVESTMENT TRUST
MODEL HERB GARDEN

The Herb Garden was redesigned by Lucy Huntingdon in 2001 and contains a huge variety of herbs that are hardy in the UK, divided according to their various properties. Here are culinary, medicinal, cosmetic and apothecary herbs and plants for pot pourri, as well as North American and Chinese herbs, a thyme lawn and some woody and bulbous plants. The design of the entire garden or any of its attractive beds could easily be copied in a domestic setting.

No.2 Witan Street 'Our Garden' by Andy Sturgeon uses blue limestone, black basalt and decking as a neutral backdrop to plants that were chosen for year-round texture and colour

Fruit Demonstration Gardens *See p26.*

Weather Hill

Taking its name from the meteorological station that once stood at its top, this gently sloping hill is home to many unusual and distinctive specimen trees, such as the fossil tree *Ginkgo biloba*. A collection of small and medium-sized garden trees has also been planted here to show how they provide attractive

Winter bark A small stand of *Betula albosinensis* var. *septentrionalis* on Weather Hill reveals beautifully peeling bark

bark, flower, fruit and leaf interest through the year. In early summer, *Cornus kousa* var. *chinensis* with its creamy pink-tinged bracts is quite spectacular and a recently planted grove of over 25 *Cornus* cultivars illustrates the many charms of the dogwoods. There are several flowering cherries, including *Prunus* 'Accolade', as well as *Sorbus* cultivars, such as S. 'Wilfrid Fox' with its marble-like green fruits. In winter, birches reveal their beautiful barks. Thousands of bulbs flower in succession to extend the season of interest.

BOWES-LYON ROSE GARDEN

This innovative project, planned with David Austin Roses and Harkness Roses and started in late 2007, replaces the old rose borders and catenary at the southern side of Weather Hill. The redevelopment involves cleaning the soil (bioremediation) in 2008 by planting *Tagetes*, then replanting in 2009 with pest- and disease-resistant, repeat-flowering roses, including climbers and ramblers. The new garden has been designed to be contemporary in style, inspire with its planting, demonstrate best environmental practice and encourage biodiversity. The design incorporates the Pavilion, built to commemorate Sir David Bowes-Lyon (RHS President 1953–61), and has a broad range of companion planting, including bulbs, *Clematis viticella* hybrids, perennials and evergreen shrubs and topiary.

Summer splendour (*Above*) The 5cm-long bracts of *Cornus kousa* var. *chinensis* are creamy-white in early summer, then white and lastly red-pink

Late spring (*Right*) An exuberant drift of *Allium* 'Gladiator', enjoying the sun on the southern edge of Weather Hill

Modern classic *Rosa* Brother Cadfael, an English rose bred by David Austin, is one of the cultivars included in the new Bowes-Lyon Rose Garden

Good practice will take account of trials of deadheading techniques carried out by Wisley, in conjunction with the Royal National Rose Society. Large-flowered and cluster-flowered bush roses, better known as hybrid teas and floribundas, were deadheaded using three different methods. First was traditional pruning, cutting back to three leaf axils with secateurs; second, using secateurs to cut to the first leaf axil; third, the revolutionary idea of snapping off the dead flower at the slightly swollen part (abscission layer) of the stem just below the flower stalk. Snapping off proved the most successful, with roses bearing more flowers and producing their next flushes sooner.

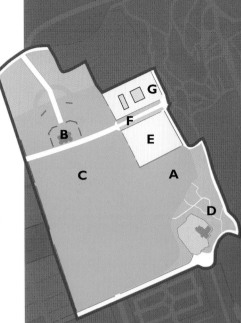

WEATHER HILL

A *Cornus* grove

B Bowes-Lyon Pavilion

C Site of Bowes-Lyon Rose Garden

D Bowles Corner

E Model Vegetable Garden

F Monocot Borders

G Alpine Display Houses

Highlights

» Winter–spring: Bowles Corner, part of NCCPG National Plant Collections of *Crocus* & *Galanthus* (see p39)

» Summer–autumn: Monocot Borders

» Year-round: Alpine Houses, Model Vegetable Garden, Weather Hill

Weather Hill

Monocot Borders Head-high flower spikes are produced in late summer by *Yucca gloriosa* 'Variegata'

BOWLES CORNER

To the east of the Model Vegetable Garden, at the bottom of Weather Hill, is the original home of George Fergusson Wilson, 'Oakwood House', which is now used as staff offices. Between the front of the house and the top of the Alpine Meadow is a small area dedicated to the great gardener, E A Bowles. He enjoyed a long association with the Society, from his election to Council in 1908 until his death in 1954. He had a penchant for what he called 'demented' plants, those not of normal habit or appearance, and some are planted here. In spring, crocuses and colchicums (another of Bowles' interests) blanket the ground under the trees.

MODEL VEGETABLE GARDEN

This is one of Wisley's main practical demonstration areas, teaching both students and visitors old and new techniques and methods of vegetable production. A mouth-watering array of 50 principal types of vegetables (in all, about 350 cultivars) are laid out in a range of growing situations. A typical, allotment-sized plot is cropped to serve a family's needs through the year. You can also pick up ideas for growing vegetables in a limited space or in tubs and troughs as a patio garden. Other features include a small potager (ornamental kitchen garden), two 3 x 3m 'Grow Your Own' plots, and a raised bed that allows easier access.

Smaller plots demonstrate some principles of organic gardening, and narrow beds, only 1.2m wide, show how you can get the most use from the soil without compacting it, as well as how you can work more conveniently. Raised beds containing highly fertile soil are useful for intensive vegetable growing. Tender subjects, such as aubergines, chillies, peppers and tomatoes, as well as early crops, are grown under the protection of a greenhouse, frames, cloches and fleece, often in conjunction with mulches to minimise weeding.

All waste from the Model Vegetable Garden is recycled in a range of compost bins at the bottom of the garden. The crops are rotated annually under a three- or four-year crop rotation scheme.

Summer squash Gather young fruits before they get too large, to get the best flavour and texture and to encourage the plant to keep fruiting

MONOCOT BORDERS

Bordering a pathway between the Alpine Display Houses and Model Vegetable Garden are the Monocot Borders. These concentrate on one of the two great classes of flowering plants – the monocotyledons. These plants all share certain physical characteristics: they have only one seed leaf, parallel leaf veins, flowers with three, or multiples of three, petals and often sword-like leaves. Most plants, such as crocosmias, grasses and kniphofias, that you see in these borders are at their best in late summer and autumn. The borders were last refreshed in 2004.

Model Vegetable Garden
(*Above*) A wide variety of vegetables, both hardy and tender, are grown throughout the year in the garden; different cultivars may be seen from year to year

Red chard (*Far left*) The deeply veined, bold leaves of chard make it an excellent plant for a potager, or ornamental vegetable garden

Compost bins (*Left*) An important part of any vegetable garden is the compost bin: it turns the waste from the garden into a valuable organic material that improves soil structure, adds nutrients and holds in moisture

Weather Hill

ALPINE DISPLAY HOUSES

True alpine (montane) plants have adapted to cope with a harsh existence high on the mountainside. They anchor themselves in small spaces between the rocks, using long roots that search for water and nutrients in the sparse soil, and keep low to the ground to avoid wind turbulence. Winter snows insulate the plants, keeping them just above freezing point. To grow alpines successfully in the UK it is essential to replicate their natural habitats. True alpines like to stay cool, while Mediterranean-climate 'alpines' tolerate summer wet, but not winter wet or frost, and are adapted to limit moisture loss through transpiration in summer. You can see plants of both kinds in the Alpine Display Houses and on the outdoor features.

Alpine Display House Kindly donated by Alitex Ltd and formally opened in 2008, this display house contains representatives of a wide range of species and cultivars from all over the world, including part of the NCCPG National *Crocus* Collection (*see opposite*). The plants are kept in pots of very sharply draining, gritty compost and are sunk into beds of sand, which acts as insulation and protects the growing medium from overheating or freezing. This also aids watering, since water is transferred from damp sand to the pot. Throughout the year, the plants are constantly changed, so that the visitor can see more plants from the larger Wisley collection at their peaks of flower and foliage. It also allows the plants to rest.

Landscape Alpine House Rebuilt in 1995–6 with generous financial assistance from the Hendry Bequest Fund, this house has a simulated dry gully running between 1.5m-high miniature cliffs that illustrate several rock types and provide niches for difficult-to-please alpines.

OUTSIDE THE ALPINE DISPLAY HOUSES

Surrounding the Alpine Display Houses is a range of planted drystone walls made from Sussex sandstone and Purbeck limestone, as well as tufa walls. A rotating collection of hypertufa sinks and troughs are planted with a range of alpines that may be

Oxalis versicolor (*top left*)
Primula auricula 'Harry Hotspur' (*centre left*)
Lewisia cotyledon hybrid (*bottom left*)

Ringing the changes (*Right*)
The displays in the alpine houses are regularly changed so that the plants are seen at their best and more varieties can be shown

grown outdoors successfully by any gardener with a limited space. There are some new beds that group South American, South African and European species by their origins, and in naturalistic plantings. Sand beds are planted with drought-tolerant alpines (xerophytes) that may be grown in gardens where water conservation is a concern.

NCCPG NATIONAL PLANT COLLECTION

Crocus A large drift of hardy crocuses is a welcome and familiar sight in public parks and gardens, but there are also many that will not survive if grown outside. *Crocus* species originate from parts of Europe, North Africa, the Middle East and Asia and are found growing low on mountainsides, in woodland or meadows. The jewel-bright species that are found in montane areas of Central Europe need the protection of a frame or alpine house since they are unable to cope with wet weather and need a very dry summer.

Over 115 of the 125 species and subspecies known in the wild and 68 cultivars are held in the NCCPG National *Crocus* Collection at Wisley. You can see spring-, autumn- and winter-flowering plants from the collection in their turns in the Alpine Display Houses. Some species of *Crocus* are naturalised in the Alpine Meadow (*see p37*).

A number of snowdrops from the NCCPG National *Galanthus* Collection are displayed, when in flower, in the Alpine House (for more information about the NCCPG National Plant Collections, *see p51*.)

Scented crocus *Crocus sieberi* 'Bowles' White' is one of the plants in Wisley's NCCPG National *Crocus* Collection; it produces 2–3cm flowers in late winter and early spring

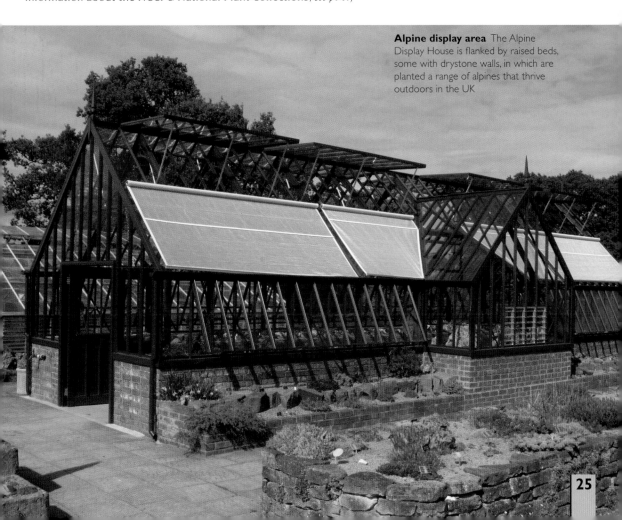

Alpine display area The Alpine Display House is flanked by raised beds, some with drystone walls, in which are planted a range of alpines that thrive outdoors in the UK

Fruit Field & Jubilee Arboretum

On your way to the Fruit Field, visit the Fruit Demonstration Gardens. These demonstrate many ways of obtaining a good yield from hardy fruits in a small garden. Modern dwarfing rootstocks are used for apples and pears, and trees are trained as spindle bushes, cordons, espaliers, fans and pyramids. Soft fruits are grown too, with some standards of red and white currants and gooseberries. There is an allotment garden with fruits, vegetables and cut flowers in raised beds and a polythene tunnel for early produce. Another garden is managed with cultivars and techniques suited to organic production. One of the most recent additions is a fruit and vegetable garden to support the RHS 'Grow Your Own' campaign.

Jubilee Arboretum There is a collection of ornamental apples (*Malus*) that give a fine show of spring blossom

FRUIT FIELD

The Society has always held an outstanding fruit collection, beginning with one at the RHS garden in Chiswick in the 19th century. Today the Fruit Field is a living library of over 1,300 different fruit cultivars, including 175 pear, 100 plum and almost 700 apple cultivars – it is the most accessible collection of its type in the UK. Many of the immaculately trained apple trees were planted in the 1950s and are grouped into eating and cooking apples, arranged according to their season of ripening. Recent plantings are on semi-dwarfing rootstocks in forms suitable for a domestic garden. A collection of cider apples was added in 1999.

You can also see strawberries, quinces, gooseberries, raspberries, black, red and white currants, various hybrid berries and nuts in the Fruit Field, as well as trials of soft fruit. The two parallel fences at the

Restricted tree forms Training fruit trees on a wall or fence saves space and makes it easier to protect crops such as cherries and peaches against damage from insects, birds and frosts

Fruitful harvest Ripening wild blackberries (*above left*), apple 'Kidd's Orange Red' (*above centre*) and white bullaces (*above right*)

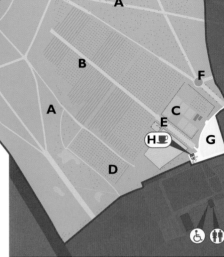

eastern approach to the field support restricted tree forms suitable for wall training, such as fans and espaliers. There is also a small vine collection, with dessert and wine-making cultivars of outdoor grapes.

A collection of cherries on dwarfing rootstocks was added on the southern side of the field in 2003 and a small vineyard in 2004. Vines of the white wine grapes 'Phönix' and 'Orion' are trained following the double Guyot system; wine from them is sold in the Wisley shop. A block of 40 disease-resistant apple cultivars are managed organically and interplanted with cornfield annuals to attract beneficial insects.

JUBILEE ARBORETUM

This was created to commemorate the Queen's Silver Jubilee in 1977. You can find almost 1,000 trees from over 90 different genera here. One of the main purposes of the Arboretum is to enable visitors to compare and contrast different groups, in a living reference library. In the first group, trees are arranged according to the season of interest; in the second, on the basis of common characteristics such as shape, colour and the type of foliage and flower; in the third, you can see all the species and cultivars of a particular genus.

The end of winter is heralded by large drifts of naturalised *Narcissus*, grown from 17,000 bulbs donated in 1998 by the Daffodil Society to celebrate its centenary.

FRUIT MOUNT

A mount is an artificial hill created to provide vistas over a garden and its surroundings. It originated in the 14th century and was a favourite feature in the 18th-century garden landscape. The Wisley Fruit Mount was planted originally by staff from all departments of the RHS as a Millennium project; it was rebuilt in 2007, using some of the soil excavated from the glasshouse lake. The Mount is almost 4m high and offers superb views over the Fruit Field, over the Glasshouse Borders down to the Glasshouse and its lake, and to the Wey valley beyond. The spiralling path is planted with apples that are ordered by date of origin, with the oldest at the top, and a groundcover of myrtle (*Myrtus communis* subsp. *tarentina*). An avenue of cider apples approaches from the east.

Highlights

» Spring: fruit blossom, *Narcissus*

» Spring–autumn: Fruit Field, Fruit Demonstration Garden

» Year round: Jubilee Arboretum

Fruit Mount, after rebuilding

The Glasshouse

The magnificent new Glasshouse, funded largely by private donations as well as £2.5 million from the RHS, was built to celebrate the RHS Bicentenary and opened in June 2007 by the Queen. It provides a dramatic focal point in the western part of the garden and a perfect showcase for Wisley's world-class collection of glasshouse plants; the design concept for the location and lake was originated by landscape architect Hal Moggridge. The project also gave an opportunity to extend the landscaping in the garden and construct spacious growing and educational facilities.

GLASSHOUSE BORDERS

Leading down from the Fruit Mount (*see p27*), these borders form a spectacular approach to the Glasshouse. Over 150m long and 11m wide, they are backed by shrubs and contained by an avenue of *Cornus kousa* var. *chinensis* 'Wisley Queen'. The borders were originally designed by the Dutch plantsman and designer Piet Oudolf to embrace a modern approach to naturalistic perennial planting.

Over 16,000 perennials and grasses were used in 2000 in the initial arrangement of more than 30 diagonal 'rivers' of three or four cultivars. Inspired by prairie plantings, Oudolf chose species and cultivars with an open, airy feel to give the impression of walking in a meadow. The borders look attractive for much of the year and are cut down only in late January. In winter, the grasses and perennial stems provide a haven for birds and wildlife.

GLASSHOUSE GARDEN

The garden was designed by Tom Stuart-Smith and provides an impressive setting for the new building; it forms a large amphitheatre, centred on the Glasshouse and the lake, and bounded by a series of beech (*Fagus sylvatica*) hedges. Within the concentric paths and beds, the mainly perennial planting changes in character to reflect and draw together the different areas of Wisley that surround it. A woodland

Architecture The award-winning design of the Glasshouse allows as much light as possible to reach the plants

Fine vista The Glasshouse viewed from the Fruit Mount at the top of the Glasshouse Borders in early summer

Glasshouse lake This stretch of water has not been planted so that its unbroken surface can act as a perfect mirror for the soaring curves of the glasshouse

element to the east echoes the Wild Garden (*pp*38–9) and is punctuated by geometric panels of monocultural planting. To the south, simple blocks of perennials in pink, mauve and purple continue the theme of the Glasshouse Borders, whereas to the west, the prairie style of the beds becomes more complex and informal.

The garden encloses an elegant lake that also has environmental benefits: it is a water reservoir, with a capacity of 1.3 million gallons, for harvesting water from the Glasshouse roof for irrigation purposes.

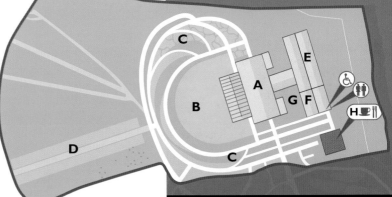

THE GLASSHOUSE

A	Glasshouse
B	Lake
C	Glasshouse Garden
D	Glasshouse Borders
E	Service Greenhouses
F	Clore Learning Centre
G	Teaching Garden
H	Glasshouse Café

Highlights

» Spring–autumn: Glasshouse Borders & Garden

» Year-round: Glasshouse display

» Seasonal: rotating exhibits in Horticultural Theatre

Glasshouse Garden (*Above*) The prairie style of the borders blends seamlessly into the naturalistic planting in curving beds that surround the lake

Statement of gratitude The names of the many societies and RHS members who contributed to the glasshouse project are engraved on these glass panels; major donors are recorded inside the Glasshouse

The Glasshouse

Moist Temperate Zone The waterfall and bold foliage create a subtropical atmosphere: green foliage of *Heliconia scheidiana* and coppery leaves of *Ensete ventricosum* 'Maurelii' from the banana family overshadow the leaves of the Asian giant taro (*Alocasia macrorrhiza*)

THE GLASSHOUSE

This cathedral-like building, designed by architect Peter van de Toorn Vrijthoff, consists mainly of curved sheets of tempered glass – 11,000sq metres weighing 110 tonnes. The glass soars to 12m high, covers an area equal in size to ten tennis courts and allows in 80 per cent of the available light. Inside, different computer-controlled environments are maintained in the same space by adjusting light, heat, ventilation, shading, energy conservation, nutrition and irrigation in specific areas. Thermal screens retain heat at night and control light levels during the day while fogging sprayers maintain humidity.

There are three main climatic zones, which create conditions that are suitable for plants from around the world. The landscaping within the Glasshouse uses 'rock' made from glass-reinforced concrete moulded from natural outcrops. As you follow the path through the Glasshouse, the environment and climate changes gradually, so that you can take a tour through the world of plants. Here you can see an extensive and diverse range of wild species and garden hybrids and cultivars, many of them beautiful and exotic, including hundreds of orchids and many cultivars of *Begonia*. The display embraces more than 5,000 taxa of tender plants – some of them difficult to grow, some of them rare, vulnerable or endangered species.

The Glasshouse collection provides a reservoir for breeding programmes and glasshouse trials, but also offers many examples of plants, such as *Caladium bicolor*, *Echinocactus grusonii*, *Streptocarpus* hybrids and many orchid hybrids including *Phalaenopsis*, which may be grown in a conservatory or domestic greenhouse or as houseplants.

MOIST TEMPERATE ZONE

On the shadier, east side of the Glasshouse, it is heated to 8–12°C and kept humid with a plentiful water supply. Here you can see natives of temperate forests from South America and Australasia, as well as parts of Cornwall and Scotland. A groundcover of ferns and other plants creeps beneath the understorey of shrubs and epiphytes, which in turn are shaded by a canopy of trees and tree ferns. This naturalistic planting blends species from across the world: Australasian tree ferns, South American climbers, pitcher plants from North American bogs, South African lilies and Asian gingers.

A waterfall serves as an impressive focal point as well as offering different planting opportunities because of the subtle changes in growing conditions on the adjacent rock face. The moisture held beneath the canopies of tree ferns in shaded areas nearby creates a cloud-forest atmosphere and even more planting possibilities.

DRY TEMPERATE ZONE

This scree and rock-strewn landscape on the sunny, west side of Glasshouse is also heated to 8–12°C, but mimics dry semi-arid and desert environments. As in the wild, it appears sparsely planted but contains a rich diversity of tough, slow-growing, frequently prickly and strangely beautiful plants. The plants are adapted to conserve every drop of moisture. There are many desert cacti and succulents and other drought-tolerant plants from countries as far apart as Chile, South Africa and Madagascar to the Canary Islands and Australia.

Pitcher plant This large carnivorous plant in the Moist Temperate Zone is *Sarracenia minor* 'Okee Giant'. It lures its insect prey partly by illuminating the interior of the pitcher with light entering through the translucent, white patches below the hood

Haageocereus multangularis   *Pachypodium lamerei*   *Mammillaria senilis*

Dry Temperate Zone In this stony setting, cacti are grown together with other succulents from the Americas, such as *Agave attenuata*, here growing out of the rockface

Moth orchid The veined blooms of *Phalaenopsis* Brother Lancer (*below left*) are produced over several months

Tropical waterlily The flowers of this *Nymphaea* 'Director George T. Moore' (*below centre left*) can be 25cm across

Slipper orchid Many orchids from this genus, *Paphiopedilum* (*below centre*), are terrestrial and grow in tropical Asia

Flamingo flower *Anthurium* 'Red Love' (*below right*) is a cultivar of a species that is native to Ecuador and Colombia, where it grows in leaf litter on the forest floor

The Glasshouse

TROPICAL ZONE

This area overlooks the lake and is provided with a minimum night temperature of 20°C and a relative humidity of about 70 per cent, to create an environment that is similar to a tropical rainforest. Such conditions promote fast growth, huge leaf sizes and extravagant, vividly hued flowers. The lush planting includes bananas, bromeliads, palm trees and fast-growing climbers, as well as familiar houseplants growing to their natural sizes, such as the Swiss cheese plant (*Monstera deliciosa*) and giant maidenhair fern (*Adiantum trapeziforme*). A viewing platform allows you to get up among the tree canopy.

A jungle pool, heated to 28°C, is stocked with tropical waterlilies and other aquatic and wetland plants; some are cultivars rather than wild species for a more dramatic display. There are also plantings from equatorial mountain habitats.

The Tropical Zone provides a home for many orchids from the Wisley collection; the *Orchidaceae* is the world's large family of flowering plants and many are tree dwellers. Plants from the orchid collection are rotated to create a constantly changing display.

Tropical Zone A banana, *Musa* x *paradisiaca*, shades a temporary display of orange-flowered bromeliads

HORTICULTURAL THEATRE

Continually changing displays of plants are staged here at the centre of the Glasshouse to provide inspiration and practical ideas for gardeners. Plants such as chrysanthemums, fuchsias, poinsettias and winter bulbs are brought from the service greenhouses into the theatre when they reach their full magnificence.

ROOT ZONE

An exciting, interactive learning area in an underground cavern demonstrates the vital importance of roots to plants, soil structure, soil organisms and the atmosphere. You can also find out how roots grow, how they can suffer damage, and how they supply us with resources such as food, medicine and dyes.

Horticultural Theatre Autumn fireworks are provided by cascade and charm chrysanthemums

BEYOND THE GLASSHOUSE

The service greenhouses are working glasshouses that run between the Glasshouse and Clore Learning Centre. They enable the staff to provide a constant supply of new plants grown to perfection for the display glasshouses. They are generally not accessible to the general public, but you can view one of them from the Glasshouse and see works in progress.

Also visible from the Glasshouse are the environmentally sustainable Teaching Garden, designed by Cleve West, and the Clore Learning Centre. Together, these facilities enable the RHS to deliver a first-class learning experience to children and adults alike (for more details, *see pp52–3*).

Tropical Zone (*Left*) Pools like this occur in natural rainforests, but the planting here includes cultivars to bring more drama and colour to the display

Root Zone Explore the subterranean, and usually forgotten, world of plant roots and find out how important roots are to plant health and soil structure

Rock Garden & Alpine Meadow Only

a few years after Wisley was given to the Society, the first major project – the creation of the rock garden – began. It was a huge engineering project and was built by James Pulham & Sons, specialists in large-scale rock gardens, to designs by the landscape

Grotto Ferns guarding the entrance are *Matteuccia struthiopteris* (foreground) and *Osmunda cinnamomea* (centre left); *Rodgersia podophylla* clothes the roof

architect, Edward White. The natural appearance of the garden is said to have been achieved by positioning the Sussex sandstone blocks to the same orientation as they were before they were quarried. The steep slope faces north and suits many plants that prefer a cool, shady spot, while there is room on the more exposed outcrops for sun-loving plants. The north-facing aspect is cold and damp in the winter with low light levels and many of the alpines need sharp drainage and skilful management to survive.

Maintaining this magnificent bank is a continual battle against the combination of light sandy soil, natural underground springs and the forces of gravity. The last major renovation was in 2004, when the dramatic waterfall with its Japanese-style landscape, designed by Professor Masao Fukuhara, was constructed.

Numerous small paths lead down and around the rocky outcroppings and little pools that are linked by streams and cascades; the water eventually flows into the Long Ponds at the bottom. Some original features still exist, including a grotto – towards the western end of the Rock Garden – and the rustic bridge over the Long Ponds.

Hardy beauty (Above) *Cyclamen coum*, a popular rock-garden plant, originates from the Caucasus and flowers from midwinter into spring

Rock Garden Bank A mixture of shrubs and trees, herbaceous plants and bulbs are combined with alpine plants to ensure that the bank has something of interest all year round

Waterfall This was designed to marry the Japanese style of rock arrangement with the garden's original features

Wisteria floribunda 'Multijuga' has adorned this bridge, and its predecessor, for almost a century, trailing its graceful, lilac-blue and purple tassles in the water.

In the Rock Garden, you can see a wide range of plants from every alpine region of the world, combined with herbaceous perennials, marginal and aquatic plants. It has taken a long process of trial and error to discover what plants will grow where, but the garden now offers colour and interest all year round. The local climate suits marginally hardy plants, but an experimental bed has recently been installed to try out new plantings of South African alpines.

ROCK GARDEN & ALPINE MEADOW

A Rock Garden Bank
B Long Ponds
C Alpine Meadow
D Path to Glasshouse

Highlights

» Spring: Alpine Meadow, parts of NCCPG National Plant Collections of *Crocus* & *Epimedium*

» Spring–autumn: Rock Garden, Long Ponds

» Autumn: Alpine Meadow

» Winter: parts of NCCPG National Plant Collection of *Galanthus* (snowdrops)

Long Ponds Yellow flag (*Iris pseudacorus*) and Asian candelabra primulas thrive in the moist soil on the banks of the ponds

Rock Garden & Alpine Meadow

ALPINE MEADOW

During March and April, the grassy slope next to the Rock Garden Bank is transformed into a sheet of sulphur-yellow by thousands of naturalised hoop-petticoat daffodils (*Narcissus bulbocodium*). These daffodils and their partners, dogs-tooth violets (*Erythronium dens-canis*), snakeshead fritillaries (*Fritillaria meleagris*) and primulas, have perfect conditions to thrive in the meadow. Once the bulbs finish flowering, the grass is left uncut until late summer so that the orchid and other seeds can drop to the soil and butterflies and other insects are provided with a food supply and shelter. The meadow is mown closely before autumn-flowering crocuses (*Crocus speciosus*) appear.

Look for species from the NCCPG National *Crocus* Collection (*see p25*) in the Alpine Meadow: C. *tommasinianus* and C. *vernus* flower in spring and C. *nudiflorus*, C. *pulchellus* and C. *speciosus* in autumn. There are also some snowdrops from the NCCPG National *Galanthus* Collection (*see p39*) to be seen in the meadow in late winter.

Alpine Meadow This is at its peak in mid-spring, when the hoop petticoat daffodils (*Narcissus bulbocodium*) flower

NCCPG NATIONAL COLLECTION

Epimediums are tough, slow-growing but long-lived. They are happiest in shaded areas growing under trees and shrubs and their evergreen or deciduous heart-shaped leaves provide good ground cover. The Wisley collection comprises 39 species and subspecies, with 44 different cultivars. The smaller epimediums, such as E. *grandiflorum*, of the collection are happiest in the Rock Garden, while the Wild Garden (*see pp38–9*) offers an ideal habitat for the larger epimediums. In spring, look out for their delicate flowers, which are suspended above the leaves on thin, wiry stems. (For more information about the NCCPG National Plant Collections, *see p51*.)

Epimedium This species, *Epimedium leptorrhizum*, is a slowly spreading evergreen and 12–30cm tall

Skunk cabbage (*Lysichiton camtschatcensis*)   Siberian iris (*Iris sibirica* 'Heavenly Blue')   *Darmera peltata*

Wild Garden

The spirit of George Fergusson Wilson's original garden lives on in the Wild Garden. This is the most historic part of Wisley and, although much altered, it remains true to his ethos of 'growing difficult plants successfully' in a naturalistic style. In his notebooks, Wilson recorded almost 22,000 separate plantings in

Woodland colour Foliage plants such as *Rodgersia pinnata* (*left in foreground*) combine with colourful woodland perennials such as *Ligularia* and skunk cabbage (*Lysichiton*)

'Oakwood' (as it was then called) from 1878 until his death in 1902. The soil in the Wild Garden is peaty and more moisture-retentive than elsewhere in Wisley, and was ideal for growing woodland plants – until storms depleted the tree canopy.

New plantings are gradually re-forming the canopy and, on the ground, the area is being restocked with an immense variety of hostas, primulas, trilliums and the many other woodlanders that find the high water table and fertile soil so conducive to their growth. As in natural woodland, lower-growing trees and shrubs fill in the middle layer of vegetation and in spring, camellias, magnolias, rhododendrons and bulbs provide glorious spring colour, while through autumn assorted trees and shrubs display rich shades of red and orange. In winter, the vivid, spidery flowers of witch hazel (*Hamamelis*) scent the air.

In 1990, a bamboo walk was introduced on the exposed southwest flank to filter the wind and it has become a great favourite with young visitors, who can walk through bamboo stands that tower up to 6–9m. There are over 30 different species and cultivars of bamboo in the area.

NCCPG NATIONAL PLANT COLLECTION

Galanthus Surprisingly, the common name of *Galanthus*, snowdrop, derives not from its winter flowering but the German word *schneetropfen*, describing pendants or earrings that were fashionable in the 16th and 17th centuries. Hundreds of snowdrops now exist, each with a difference – sometimes subtle, sometimes obvious – that provides a clue to its full name.

In the NCCPG National Plant Collection at Wisley, there are 16–19 different species (depending on botanical classification) and more than 100 cultivars. Such a large collection means that you can look at several varieties as they grow next to each other and compare differences in height, flower size and in the shape, size, position and colour of the green or yellow-green markings on the inner petals. The positions and shapes of emerging leaves also differ.

A large collection of *Galanthus nivalis* cultivars carpets the Wild Garden and there are also plantings of G. *elwesii* var. *monostictus*. Others may be found on Battleston Hill (*see pp*12–13) or in the Rock Garden (*see pp*34–7). Part of the collection is not on public display, but some of the more special snowdrops are displayed in the Alpine Display Houses (*see pp*24–5) when they are in flower.

There are also some plants from the NCCPG National E*pimedium* Collection (*see p37*) to be seen around the garden in spring. (For more information about the NCCPG National Plant Collections, *see p51*.)

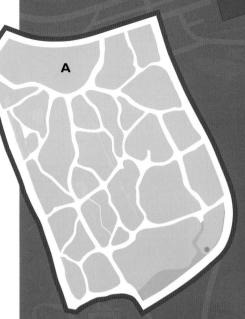

A

Summer perennials (*Left*)
Fluffy pink spikes of astilbes and magenta flowers of *Geranium psilostemon* brighten the floor of the Wild Garden in early summer

WILD GARDEN

A Bamboo walk

Highlights

» Spring–summer: bulbs, shrubs and perennials, part of NCCPG National *Epimedium* Collection

» Autumn: foliage

» Winter: bark, snowdrops

» Year-round: bamboo walk

Arum lily (*Above*) Stately stands of *Zantedeschia aethiopica* 'Crowborough' thrive in the moist soil by the watersides

Osmunda regalis (royal fern)

Galanthus elwesii (snowdrop)

Seven Acres

Originally, Seven Acres was rough pastureland and thought to be useless for cultivation until, in the 1920s, an iron pan was discovered just below the soil surface. Once the pan had been broken up, plant roots could at last reach the water table and a range of specimen trees was planted. The smaller of the two

Late autumn The fine, palm-shaped leaves of the sweet gum (*Liquidambar styraciflua*) are softly elegant in summer and then veined and flushed purple-red in autumn before they fall

ponds (known as the Round Pond) started life in the early years of Wisley as a source of gravel for garden paths and has remained as a water feature ever since. In 2000–2001, the two pond areas were redesigned. A grass causeway now separates the Lake from the Round Pond, but a small weir generated by a self-circulating water feature in the lake gives the impression that the two are connected.

Planting around the pond and lake focuses on four seasonal themes: summer at the eastern end, spring to the west, and autumn and winter drifting throughout. During spring, thousands of daffodils (*Narcissus*) and grape hyacinths (*Muscari*) colour both the lawns and beds. In autumn, many of the trees, such as *Nyssa sylvatica* 'Wisley Bonfire', glow with vibrant foliage. Sculptures of two dancing cranes, by Gail Runyon Perry, seem poised on the water of the lake.

GRASS BORDER

This border leads along the edge of Seven Acres from the lake and pond to the Conservatory Café and Terrace Restaurant. Many of the

Chinese Pavilion Originally built in the style of a Chinese temple for a garden exhibit at the 2005 Hampton Court Palace Flower Show, the pavilion sits on the edge of the Lake

Round Pond A view across the Pond to the summerhouse, which shelters among the trees and shrubs on the western edge of Seven Acres

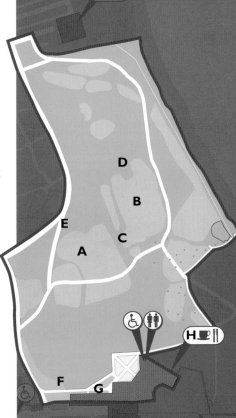

Grass Border Among the grasses here are *Stipa calamagrostis* in the foreground and the tall pampas grass *Cortaderia selloana* in the background, with purple-flowered *Miscanthus sinensis* 'Pünktchen' towards the back of the border

graceful grasses here reach 2.2–2.5m and provide an excellent example of large-scale group plantings. Herbaceous perennials and annual plants, such as agapanthus, kniphofias and bearded irises, add colour and contrast. A useful collection of grasses suitable for a small garden can be seen by the restaurant. The border is mulched with 'rivers' of pebbles running across gravel.

SEVEN ACRES

A	Round Pond
B	Lake
C	Causeway
D	Chinese pavilion
E	Summerhouse
F	Grass Border
G	Wisley Garden Library
H	Conservatory Café & Terrace Restaurant

Highlights

» Spring: bulbs, waterside planting on western edge

» Summer: waterside planting on eastern edge

» Autumn: tree foliage, waterside planting

» Summer–winter: Grass Border, waterside planting

» Winter: stem colour on eastern edge

Pinetum & Howard's Field
This is a very tranquil area of the garden, bounded on one side by the local Wisley Lane and on the other by the River Wey. The Pinetum is named after the towering pines first planted by George Fergusson Wilson around 1898. Now it is a collection of mainly coniferous trees, such

as Pinus nigra and Thuja plicata 'Zebrina', as well as a fine monkey puzzle (Araucaria araucana). Spring and autumn colour is provided by shrubs and deciduous trees, for example Japanese maples (Acer palmatum) and flowering dogwoods (Cornus), as well as bulbs such as daffodils (Narcissus). A number of the original conifers are champion trees (see panel, opposite). In the western corner of the pinetum is a platform overlooking the river – a good place for spotting kingfishers.

Autumn colour The evergreen of the conifers in the Pinetum is leavened with autumn foliage of deciduous trees such as Acer palmatum

HOWARD'S FIELD
Visitors who journey to this quiet, contemplative clearing are richly rewarded. Huge, cushion-like beds in luxuriant hues hold the NCCPG National Heather Collection (see opposite). There is also a collection of ornamental trees, such as birch (Betula), catalpa, red oak (Quercus rubra) and cherry (Prunus), while at the far end of the field there is a trial of Buddleja davidii and of Indigofera, which flower from summer to autumn.

WILDLIFE CONSERVATION AREA
This precious resource on the banks of the river Wey was established on about three acres of wooded floodplain in 1998, creating an oxbow

Wildlife Conservation Area
Increasing numbers of birds, insects and animals are finding this a safe haven in which to breed

Giant redwood This magnificent Sequoiadendron giganteum guards the entrance to the Pinetum

lake and new distinct habitats, and is managed to encourage wildlife. It is not usually open to the public, apart from occasional, planned open days, but it can be viewed from Howard's Field.

NCCPG NATIONAL PLANT COLLECTION

Heather The collection was first established at Wisley in the 1920s and received National Plant Collection status in 1987 – the first NCCPG National Plant Collection (*see p51*) of this group. It has been located in Howard's Field since 1988 and is one of the largest collections of heathers in the British Isles, comprising over 1,000 cultivars of *Calluna*, *Daboecia* and *Erica* – the three genera collectively known as heathers.

The heather beds are generally replaced with young plants after ten years. Plants are removed with minimal disturbance, to allow new plants to benefit from the mycorrhizal (symbiotic) fungi in the remnants of the older plants' root systems.

The key to keeping heathers floriferous and compact is trimming. Winter-, spring- and summer-flowering heathers should be trimmed in spring, taking care not to cut into old wood. Taller tree heaths, cultivars of *Erica arborea*, should be left alone unless they grow too large for their allotted spaces or need rejuvenating; then they can be cut back hard in spring.

PINETUM & HOWARD'S FIELD

A	Pinetum
B	Howard's Field
C	Wildlife Conservation Area
D	NCCPG National Heather Collection
E	Conservatory Café & Terrace Restaurant
F	Viewing platform
G	Picnic area

Highlights

» Spring–autumn: deciduous shrubs and trees

» Summer–autumn: trials of *Buddleja davidii* and *Indigofera*

» Year-round: evergreens in Pinetum, NCCPG National Heather Collection

Heather bed (*Left*) The patchwork of heathers includes the purple-flowered *Daboecia cantabrica* 'Harlequin'

Champion trees

A tree may be awarded the honour of 'champion' if it is the largest recorded example of any given species. During a recent survey for the Tree Register (an organisation that keeps records of notable and ancient trees in Britain and Ireland), Wisley was acknowledged as the proud custodian of over 30 champions. Seven of the champions reside in the Pinetum and five in Howard's Field. Trees are measured both on their girth and height.

Pinetum
» *Chamaecyparis lawsoniana* 'Croftway', 12m
» *Chamaecyparis lawsoniana* 'Fletcheri', 15m
» *Chamaecyparis lawsoniana* 'Golden Wonder', 8m
» *Chamaecyparis lawsoniana* 'Lanei Aurea', one of the best golden cypresses, with a columnar habit, 19m
» x *Cupressocyparis leylandii* 'Naylor's Blue', 16.5m

» *Pinus bungeana*, 14m
» *Pinus densiflora*, a Japanese red pine with reddish coloured bark, 21m
» *Pinus* x *holfordiana*, 22m
» *Pinus ponderosa* var. *scopulorum*, 15m

Howard's Field
» *Carpinus tschonoskii*, 12m
» *Ilex aquifolium* 'J.C. van Tol', 6m
» *Prunus* x *juddii*, 10m
» *Populus* 'Oxford', 10m

History

Although the oldest extant RHS garden, Wisley was not the first of the Society's gardens. The first, small garden in Kensington, owned 1818–22, was soon abandoned for a larger garden. In 1821, just 17 years after its founding, the Horticultural Society (as it was then named) leased from the Duke of Devonshire 33 acres of ground

Botanical portraits Wisley Library holds some publications with fine printed and coloured engravings, such as these of *Camellia reticulata* from the 1827 *Botanical Register*, a 19th-century periodical (*above top*), and a cantalope melon (*above*), after an original by George Brookshaw in the *Pomona Britannica* (1812)

adjoining Chiswick House. This became a repository for plants introduced from China and the Americas by the Society's collectors David Douglas, Robert Fortune, Theodore Hartweg and John Reeves. Many of the Society's introductions were also sent to the nearby Botanical Gardens at Kew. Flower shows were also held at Chiswick, starting with annual shows 1827–30 and then with more regular shows being held from 1833.

KENSINGTON

Because of its distance from London, the Society's garden at Chiswick suffered a decrease in visitors, so in 1859 it was decided to to create a new display garden that could also be used for flower shows in a more central location. The Society's then President, Prince Albert the Prince Consort, was instrumental in the lease of 22 acres of land just south of the current Royal Albert Hall, an area now occupied by the Science Museum and Imperial College. The Prince was heavily involved in the design and development of the garden, which was designed by William Andrews Newfield. The opening ceremony of the garden in 1861 proved to be the Prince's last public appearance in London before his death. The garden was an initial success, but problems of finance and air pollution soon beset it and it eventually closed in 1888.

During this period, the Society had expanded its experimental work at Chiswick with plant trials. Following the closure of the garden at Kensington, it was agreed that the Chiswick garden should be a school of scientific and practical horticulture and 'ornamental as well as useful'. This is a responsibility that Wisley and the other RHS gardens continue to uphold.

WISLEY

Many years were spent in searching for a larger garden 'beyond the radius of the London smoke' to replace that at Chiswick. In 1903, Sir Thomas Hanbury, a wealthy Quaker and founder of the celebrated garden of La Mortola on the Italian Riviera, presented in trust to the Society 60 acres of freehold land at Wisley in Surrey. At that time, the Society was also committed to building a new exhibition hall and offices in Vincent Square (construction work had already started) and there were heated arguments among the Fellows over whether the new hall or garden should have priority for the available funds. Sir Thomas' generous donation appeared to have come out of the blue and solved the problem at a stroke.

By May 1904, the move from Chiswick to Wisley was complete and, in July, the new headquarters at Vincent Square were officially opened by King Edward VII – both in time to mark the centenary of the Society.

The garden at Wisley had previously been known as Oakwood and was the garden of George Fergusson Wilson, a businessman, scientist, inventor, keen gardener and former Treasurer of the RHS. He bought the site in 1878 and established the 'Oakwood experimental garden', with the idea of making 'difficult plants grow successfully'. The garden acquired a reputation for its collections of gentians, Japanese irises, lilies, primulas and water plants. The present Wild Garden (*see pp*38–9) is the direct descendant of Oakwood.

Kensington 1861 Hyde Park can be glimpsed on the horizon; the green space in the centre of the park would later host the Albert Memorial

One of the first major construction works was a range of glasshouses, which occupied the site of the present canal in front of the laboratory. Built in 1905, they accommodated fruits that would not survive the harsh frosts from which Wisley has always suffered. The Rock Garden Bank was the next major construction at Wisley; it was a major engineering project and required the installation of a light railway from the nearest road (now the A3) through the Fruit Field. The Rock Garden was completed in 1911; over the years, it has undergone several restorations but remains essentially the same structure.

The Rock Garden This view, taken in 1914, of the newly planted Rock Garden is missing the now-familiar outline of the Laboratory in the distance

History

Original glasshouses Built in 1905, these occupied the area in front of the Laboratory building until the 1960s, when the canal was installed

EDUCATION

It was at Chiswick that the Society's educational work began with training student gardeners, often referred to as 'labourers'. The Society approved the furnishing of a study and lecture room and increased the number of books in the small library held there.

By 1907, a small laboratory was built at Wisley for the purpose of scientific research and as a study centre for student gardeners. To further the excellent educational work begun at Chiswick, a training course for students was set up the next year. Students paid an admission fee of five guineas for a two-year course and, after an intensive programme of study and practical experience, received a diploma granted by the Wisley School of Horticulture.

Over the last century, hundreds of students have passed through Wisley training; nowadays, students come from all over the world and are paid a training allowance for the two-year diploma course or take a one-year course option.

NEW LABORATORY

As the garden developed, so the number of staff and students increased and outgrew the small laboratory. This was incorporated into the building of the new Laboratory, a building carefully designed to appear as if the garden had been developed around it rather than preceding it. Begun in 1914 and completed in 1916, the Laboratory was designed to provide improved facilities for students and offices for the increasing number of scientific and administrative staff. It was

The Laboratory The building was nearing completion in 1915; it was modelled on vernacular buildings in Surrey to resemble a manor house

built with recycled materials from old manor houses and has walls made of Sussex and York stone. The wood panelling in the reception area, a grand staircase and stained glass panels in the windows all add to the country-house feel of the building, but away from this entrance area are well-equipped offices, as well as pathology and entomology labs and the Herbarium, library and lecture theatre.

When war broke out again in 1939, although the numbers of staff and students were greatly depleted, the garden continued to be maintained and played its own part in the war effort. Demonstrations and lectures helped amateur gardeners increase productivity of fruit and vegetables on their plots; troops also were given training in self-sufficiency; a model allotment garden demonstrated the best way of using space; vegetables likely to be in short supply were cultivated and medicinal plants and their seeds collected. Wisley also sent parcels of bulbs and vegetable and flower seeds to prisoner-of-war camps in Germany and Italy.

CONSTANT CHANGE

Development of the garden began again after the Second World War. In 1946, Battleston Hill was rejuvenated by the removal of over 200 trees and over 250 old tree stumps and replanted with rhododendrons and azaleas, which fare well in Wisley's acid soil. In 1954 to celebrate the 150th anniversary of the Society, HM Queen Elizabeth the Queen Mother, sister of the then President Sir David Bowes Lyon, opened a new student hostel named after the late Lord Aberconway (RHS President 1931–53). The model gardens began as an extension of the National Fruit Trials in 1946 and have continued to develop as examples of good horticultural practice and in recent years also of garden design.

Filming the garden In 1964 a model garden was laid out in order to film the television series 'Gardeners' Calendar'; sometimes the presenters were filmed from a helicopter

Potting shed Staff working in the old potting shed c.1960: it used to stand on the site of the Loggia, which now overlooks the Canal

Bowes-Lyon Pavilion This memorial to the Society's president Sir David Bowes Lyon, who died in 1961, was built in 1964 on Weather Hill and was intended to be a 'dignified but light and elegant structure'

The 1950s cherry-tree garden in Portsmouth Field made way for a Trials area in 1970, but the major construction projects in the 1960s and 1970s involved the replacement of the old glasshouses by the Laboratory and building of a new range of glasshouses near Portsmouth Field. This created space for the installation of the Canal and Loggia, designed by Sir Geoffrey Jellicoe and Lanning Roper. A restaurant and cafeteria were added to Aberconway House and a shop

Royal patrons

1809	First royal charter granted to Horticultural Society
1816	HM Queen Charlotte becomes first royal patron of the Horticultural Society
1858	Prince Albert becomes President
1861	The Society receives a new royal charter from Queen Victoria and becomes the Royal Horticultural Society; after Prince Albert dies, the Queen announces her wish to succeed him as President, but is dissuaded; she continues to take an active interest in the Society
1904	HM King Edward VII opens the new exhibition hall and agrees to become a joint patron with HM Queen Alexandra
1910	On accession to the throne, HM King George VI and HM Queen Mary become joint patrons; in 1928 Princess Mary opens the New Hall (now known as the Lawrence Hall)
1936	HM King George VI and HM Queen Elizabeth become royal patrons
1952	HM Queen Elizabeth II joins the Queen Mother as joint patron

Battleston Hill Here pictured before the storms of 1987 and 1990 felled about 80 per cent of the mature trees; the area was subsequently redeveloped with new plantings and a series of winding pathways

Royal visit The Queen on her first visit to Wisley to open the Jubilee Arboretum on 8 May 1978. The Queen planted a beech tree (*Fagus sylvatica* 'Dawyck Purple') to mark the opening

Silver Jubilee celebrations HRH Princess Anne toured the garden on 6 July 1977, escorted by the RHS Director Christopher Brickell

and plant centre built at the garden entrance. The Queen's Silver Jubilee (1977) was marked by the planting of an arboretum, extending southwest from Weather Hill. The 1980s and 1990s saw great storms (in October 1987 and January 1990) wreak havoc with the tree cover at Wisley, requiring massive replanting but providing the opportunity to revitalise areas with new plant collections.

Wisley is an ever-changing landscape: always ornamental, but also an educational tool demonstrating the best in horticulture. Just as Prince Albert influenced the Kensington garden, so each custodian, student, staff member or visitor influences some part of Wisley. The Wild Garden remains faithful to George Fergusson Wilson's ethos, E A Bowles' fascination for crocuses and snowdrops prompted the start of Wisley's National Plant Collections, while Lord Aberconway's love of all plants ericaceous initiated the collections of rhododendrons, azaleas and camellias, which enliven Battleston Hill each year.

After ten years of planning and three years of construction, the new Bicentenary Glasshouse was opened in 2007 by the Queen. It won the New Building Design award from Guildford Borough Council for its faultless landscaping, evoking the grand tradition of fine English great conservatories and being a wonderfully busy and energetic place for learning and looking. Having passed its centenary in 2003, Wisley continues to embrace the moods of the age while remaining a living encyclopedia of the best in horticulture.

After the storm Clearing up the devastation after the great storm of 16 October 1987 took two years

Behind the Scenes

Wisley was donated to the Society as an experimental garden and this spirit of research continues today. The majority of the Society's scientific staff are based in the Laboratory building and number among them horticulturists, botanists, taxonomists, plant pathologists and entomologists. In total there

are over 370 permanent staff at Wisley, of which approximately 90 work as garden staff and the remainder in the scientific, educational, administrative and retail departments.

HORTICULTURAL TRAINING

For over 200 years, one of the main aims of the RHS has been to train gardeners of the future. Nationally recognised professional qualifications are essential in any field and the Society's examinations have been hallmarks of excellence for over 100 years. Students have been learning their craft at RHS Garden Wisley since 1907. Every year applications for placements are received from all over the world and each year 34 student gardeners master the practice of horticulture at Wisley.

VOLUNTEERS

Many people support the RHS by becoming volunteers at one of the RHS gardens, helping with a whole range of tasks, from gardening and acting as tour guides to providing administrative support. There are over 100 volunteers at Wisley. The Society greatly appreciates and values the knowledge, enthusiasm and commitment they bring, and the volunteers find their time at the garden both enjoyable and rewarding. If you are interested in learning more about volunteering, please contact the National Co-ordinator of Volunteers at The Royal Horticultural Society, 80 Vincent Square, London SW1P 2PE.

Laboratory A team of scientific staff provide an invaluble advisory service to RHS members, as well as conducting research and building a leading botanical and horticultural reference resource

Service Greenhouses Here, plants are grown to a peak of perfection before being put on display in the Glasshouse or the open garden

SCIENCE AND ADVICE

Wisley's horticultural and scientific advisors receive over 70,000 enquiries each year from RHS members. Members may send in plants for identification, ask for advice on cultivation, choice of plants, or on dealing with pests, diseases and disorders.

Scientific research at Wisley arises from practical garden problems and focuses on troublesome pests, woody plant diseases, weed control and soil nutrition, ensuring that up-to-date and accurate information is available to the gardener. Examination of specimens in the laboratory as well as field experiments complement knowledge gained from work in the garden.

The Wisley Herbarium, a collection of over 50,000 preserved plant specimens, is invaluable for botanical reference. It specialises

Seed harvest Seedheads, from plants such as *Cardiocrinum giganteum* (*above right*) and *Iris foetidissima* (*above left*) are collected from all parts of the garden to be cleaned, dried and sorted

in garden rather than wild plants, and is supplemented by plants collected from trials and exhibited at RHS flower shows, as well as from those received from members for verification.

The RHS *Plant Finder* (Dorling Kindersley) is compiled and edited annually at Wisley by the Botany Department. As well as listing where to buy 70,000 or so plants, it is widely recognised as giving stability to, and as an authority on, the names of plants in cultivation.

SEED DEPARTMENT

This department of the Society is based at Wisley and distributes approximately 250,000 packets of seeds each year to RHS members and botanical institutions across the world. Over 1,000 UK schools that work with the RHS Education Department also receive seed. About 90 per cent of the seed is collected from the garden at Wisley. Throughout the year, seed is harvested from over 700 plant species growing in the gardens, by five members of staff and ten volunteers. The seed is then cleaned, checked for pests and diseases, and packed ready to distribute. This operation is probably the world's largest non-commercial seed distribution service.

Weather station This station is sited on the higher ground of the Fruit Field, and has been monitoring UK weather patterns for over 100 years

NCCPG NATIONAL PLANT COLLECTIONS

Over the years many plants are lost from our gardens: some fall from favour, others become diseased or virused or simply disappear. In 1978 the National Council for the Conservation of Plants and Gardens (NCCPG) was founded to conserve Britain's garden plant heritage. The NCCPG National Plant Collection Scheme was introduced in 1980 to prevent the extinction of plants by ensuring a continuing supply of genetic material from correctly identified and recorded stock.

The collections at Wisley formed some of the first National Plant Collections. Parts of some collections are in areas that are not accessible to the public, but many of the plants are grown or displayed around the garden. The current collections are of *Crocus* (*see p*25), *Epimedium* (*see p*37), *Galanthus* (snowdrops, *see p*39), heathers (*Calluna*, *Daboecia* and *Erica*, *see p*43) and rhubarb (*see p*15).

Learning with the RHS

The RHS Education Department is based at Wisley and one of its major roles is to inspire, enthuse and educate children about plants and gardening. The Society's goal is that, by 2012 and with RHS help, 80 per cent of UK primary schools will be providing their pupils with practical opportunities

Apt pupils The designer of the Teaching Garden, Cleve West, shows budding gardeners how to plant in rows

to learn how to grow plants and to garden in a sustainable way. The Campaign for School Gardening website (www.rhs.org.uk/schoolgardening) is a key resource, which provides a wealth of help and ideas for schools and pupils in order to get them gardening. It includes a benchmarking scheme that schools can work through; completion of each level results in a certificate and an award from the RHS.

School visits may be arranged with the Education Officers at Wisley. A range of exciting topics and workshops for schoolchildren of all ages is available. An amazing new educational facility has been built at Wisley, adjacent to the Glasshouse, and provides a stimulating location for learning.

THE CLORE LEARNING CENTRE

This facility is supported by the Clore Duffield Foundation to offer hands-on experience to gardeners of all abilities and ages, from primary-school age upwards. Here they can watch professional gardeners work in propagation houses and learn practical planting, propagating and other techniques in the Growing Laboratory. There is also a flexible learning space where students explore the science of plants through talks, lectures and

Teaching Garden Backed by the Clore Learning Centre, the garden was designed to be 'subtle...about science, art and drama as well as gardens'

experiments. They can even practise cooking healthily, study the Glasshouse architecture or undertake art projects.

TEACHING GARDEN

Designed by Cleve West working closely with the RHS Education Department, this garden is intended to work as a curriculum resource for adults and children. It includes a hexagonal teaching area, an environmentally sustainable garden shed with sedum roof, a fruit and vegetable area for growing healthy food, compost heaps for recycling waste, minibeast towers, and a pond and variety of habitats in order to encourage wildlife.

CONTINUING PROFESSIONAL DEVELOPMENT PROGRAMME

One-day courses at Wisley are available for all adults who wish to inspire schoolchildren about gardening. They provide support for teachers taking part in the Campaign for School Gardening and encourage the use of the outdoor classroom to teach the National Curriculum.

RHS FAMILY LEARNING

This programme offers a series of inspirational events and activities throughout the year at Wisley, hosted with the aim of getting families interested in gardening. 'Garden Explorer' packs and trails are available, to turn your visit into an exciting journey of discovery. Members of Garden Explorers can attend practical workshops that are run throughout the year (booking is necessary).

Garden explorers (*Above top*) Wisley provides a wealth of resources for horticultural adventures

Adult education (*Above*) A teaching session in the Fruit Field

GARDEN LIBRARY

The Garden Library at Wisley has excellent collections on practical gardening, garden history and design, and fruit and vegetable gardening. All garden visitors are welcome, including families – there is a good selection of gardening books for children. The library is also particularly useful to amateur and professional gardeners, and students of garden history or design.

The lending collection, available to RHS members, includes most new gardening books, including RHS titles. Browse the latest gardening magazines – over 90 titles – for the latest trends or older periodicals, for a fascinating insight into garden history. You can also search Wisley's plant database to locate specific plants in the garden. The Garden Library is situated near the restaurant and is open seven days a week.

Garden Library All visitors to Wisley are welcome at the library and librarians are on hand to offer help in using the library's resources

SCIENCE LIBRARY

Founded in 1846, this RHS staff and science library is open to the public by appointment. It has fine collections of floras, plant monographs, registers and checklists of cultivated plants. It also holds a good collection of 20th-century nursery catalogues. The library catalogue is on the RHS website at www.rhs.org.uk/libraries.

Events Through the Year

As well as the garden itself, visitors to Wisley can enjoy a variety of events in the garden. The RHS Education Department runs a full programme throughout the year of lectures, demonstrations, workshops and guided walks at the garden, which RHS members and the general public

are welcome to attend. The events cover a wide range of essential gardening topics, techniques and skills, as well as specific plants and tasks, garden design and art. There are workshops involving a variety of subjects including roses, trees and container gardening, as well as photographic workshops, flower-arranging and botanical-painting courses. Themed walks highlight special features, plants and trees that are of special interest. All courses must be booked in advance.

SEASONAL EVENTS

The seasons are celebrated at Wisley with various events that do not require booking and are free once visitors have gained entrance to the garden. In spring the garden is decked with a glory of bulbs, tree blossom and flowering shrubs – an experience not to be missed. During this vibrant time of year, a wide range of free garden events, activities and trails are provided, including celebrations for Easter.

In early summer, the RHS hosts its celebrated series of open-air concerts, with music to appeal to all tastes. Then the holiday season gets into full swing at Wisley with a delightful programme for all the family to enjoy: there are fun activities, workshops, competitions, trails and entertainment, all with a horticultural twist.

August sees another summer spectacular with the Wisley Flower Show. Stunning displays from award-winning nurseries, information and displays from the RHS Trials teams, as well as free advice for all our visitors ensures that the show is unmissable for gardeners.

As summer mellows, the garden offers up an abundant display of apples and pears, which are celebrated, along with a host of seasonal vegetables, in the popular 'Taste of Autumn' festival during October. Hearty foods and harvest festivities feature alongside apple tasting, demonstrations and children's activities. The garden meanwhile is painted with the wonderful hues and tints of autumn. Once the leaves have fallen, walks and talks continue, focusing on winter

Sculpture trail In 2007, 'Hare' by Juliet Simpson, 'Copernicus' by Teresa Martin (*above*) and 'Swansong' by Jeanne Argent (*below*) were exhibited, along with others, in the garden

delights such as tree barks, winter flowers and scents. Occasional sculpture trails, following original works placed around the garden in appropriate settings, are organised with the help of Surrey Sculpture Society (www.surreysculpture.org.uk).

GLASSHOUSE

All through the year, you can enjoy an exotic and unusual planting display in the Glasshouse regardless of the weather – as well as seasonal displays at its horticultural theatre, of plants such as lilies, pelargoniums and chrysanthemums, and spectacular displays of Christmas plants. The Glasshouse may be booked for a variety of evening events and can accommodate up to 550 guests (contact RHS Halls & Conference Centre, 020 7821 3680).

Open-air concerts (*Above left*)
Visitors can enjoy a range of music, from classical to rock, during the concert season at Wisley

Taste of autumn (*Above right*)
Gardeners of all ages admire the fruits of the harvest at the autumn festival

Wisley Flower Show The flower shows provide an opportunity to get advice from the highly knowledgeable Wisley horticulturists

Family fun Stiltwalking 'flowers' have entertained visitors to Wisley on several occasions – here they help to celebrate the newly opened Glasshouse

Facilities

Glasshouse Café

Terrace Restaurant

REFRESHMENTS

The Conservatory Café, Glasshouse Café and Terrace Restaurant are open all year, excluding Christmas Day. The Conservatory Café is a licensed self-service restaurant serving hot and cold meals and snacks, drinks and cakes; there are wooden tables and chairs outside the café that are popular for *al fresco* eating on mild and sunny days. The Glasshouse Café is also self-service, with all snacks and meals served up on environmentally friendly packaging. The Terrace Restaurant is a licensed restaurant with table service and a varied seasonal menu.

The Coffee Shop, at the entrance to the garden, serves freshly brewed coffees, teas, cold drinks, ice cream, cakes and sandwiches. The seasonal Orchard Café offers a selection of drinks, cakes, hot snacks and sandwiches.

WISLEY SHOP

The award-winning Wisley Shop has much to offer every shopper – not only is it one of the most comprehensive gardening bookshops in the world, but it also has a wide selection of inspirational gift items to suit all tastes. Items include cards and stationery and up-to-the-minute contemporary products, as well as RHS designs and timeless favourites.

PLANT CENTRE

The Wisley Plant Centre stocks over 10,000 plants, including 2,300 varieties of hardy perennials, 50 varieties of apple and 30 of potato, as well as groups of plants that are well represented in the garden and known as Wisley Collections. Staff at the Information Desk can give helpful advice. Visitors may consult with experts, sample different fruits and vegetables and take part in practical activities during various informal events held throughout the year. A wide range of bulbs, seeds and houseplants is always available, as well as a range of essential garden chemicals, composts and containers.

The Wisley Shop

Terrace outside the Conservatory Café